Benjamin Bean
Planting, Growing, Harvesting

Written by Carole Amateis
and
Melissa Amateis-Marsh

Illustrated by Randy Sides

Benjamin Bean
Planting, Growing, Harvesting
Copyright 2000 Carole Amateis and Melissa Amateis-Marsh
Broadwater, NE 69125
Illustrations copyright 2000 Randy Sides
Bayard, NE 69334

ISBN:0-7392-0505-6

Additional copies may be obtained by sending a completed order form (see back of book) along with payment to Benjamin Productions, Route 2, Box 77B, Broadwater, NE 69125.

Printed in the United States by: Morris Publishing
3212 East Highway 30 • Kearney, NE 68847
1-800-650-7888

This book is dedicated to the
American farmer.

Benjamin Bean
Planting, Growing, Harvesting

Hi. My name is Benjamin. I'm a Great Northern dry edible bean from the state of Nebraska. Today, my friends and I will be planted in Farmer Fred's field. We are so excited to finally grow into plants. Being a Great Northern bean is a great responsibility. We help feed people all over the world.

Farmer Fred drives his big tractor with the silver smokestack to the field. My buddies and I are poured into round buckets on the planter. As Farmer Fred drives slowly through the field, the planter pushes us into the ground. It feels good when I land in the soft, warm, fresh dirt, so I decide to take a nap.

Ahh, today I received a refreshing, cool shower from the big, dark rain clouds passing by. I hear Farmer Fred whistling as he walks through the field. I think I am beginning to sprout. Soon I will see my friends again!

Farmer Fred waits.

8

It's been a few days and my green leaves are beginning to poke through the soil! The sun feels wonderful on my tiny green limbs. All the other seeds are coming up, too. Farmer Fred comes to visit us to see if we're growing well. Every time we hear him whistle, our leaves perk up.

Uh oh! A nasty weed is growing beside me! I hope Farmer Fred notices him before he grows too tall and blocks the sun's warm rays from my leaves. I can hear him coming now. Maybe he will rescue me from the big, bad weed!

Yippee! Farmer Fred is using his cultivator and tractor to push fresh dirt around my feet. The dirt covered up that troublesome weed. Now it can't grow around me.

It's been a few weeks since we were planted. Buds on my leaves will soon turn to tiny, white flowers. And Farmer Fred is whistling again; I think he is excited. We are growing to be tall, handsome beans. I like it when he walks down the rows to see if the irrigation water is reaching our roots. Soon something wonderful will happen...our flowers will turn into bean pods! Only a few more weeks to go!

16

Today, I'm not feeling so good. These pesky bugs are crawling all over me. They keep biting me and I am not growing well. I hope Farmer Fred can help.

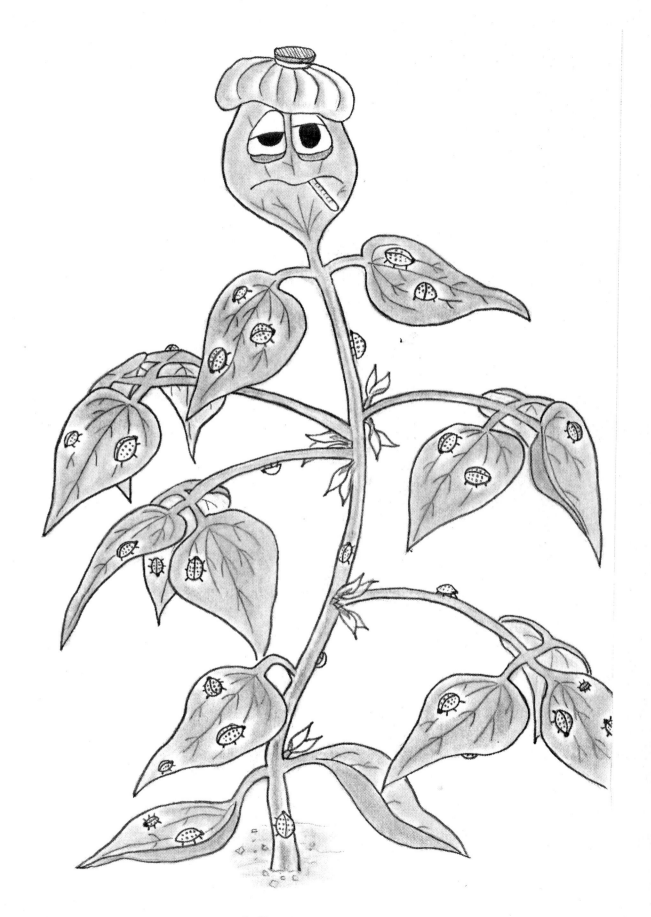

Farmer Fred's helpers are flying overhead and spraying the bugs on my leaves. Those pests are gone now, and I'm starting to feel better. I am growing stronger and forming beans in my pods.

Summer is almost over. My friends and I are starting to turn shades of yellow and brown. Some of my leaves are falling off. That means it's almost time for harvest. Farmer Fred counts all the beans in one of my pods. 1, 2, 3, 4, 5, 6.

The sun isn't even awake yet and I can hear Farmer Fred out in the field with his tractor. My leaves are all wet with dew. Farmer Fred uses his bean cutter with the sharp knives to cut our roots. We gently fall to the ground. The moisture from the dew keeps our pods from breaking.

24

Now, we will sunbathe for several days. We are laying on the ground and it's time for us to dry so Farmer Fred can pick us up with his combine. Ahh, that sun sure does feel good!

It's early September and I can hear Farmer Fred coming. The slow grinding roar of the combine is getting closer. The head of the combine uses its rollers and teeth to pick us off the dry ground. Whoa! Here I go!

28

Inside the combine, I am separated from the pods. Here I go again...I'm traveling down the auger which spits me out into a truck box. Pretty soon, my buddies and I are together again. Hooray!

Now we are going on a trip, away from the fields and the noise of the trucks and combines. Up ahead is the beanery where we will be dumped and cleaned. We'll stay in a large grain bin, and later my friends and I will be put into sacks.

While we are being weighed at the beanery, Farmer Fred reaches into the truck box and picks me up. Looking me over, he says,

"You're a perfectly-shaped Great Northern. I'm going to keep you and show you to my family."

He carefully puts me in his shirt pocket.

34

Wow! This is great! I am traveling around with Farmer Fred. Back at the farmhouse, he sets me on a special wooden shelf in the kitchen. I wonder what adventures we'll have next?

Benjamin's Buzz Words

cultivator	irrigation
combine	harvest
bean pod	beanery
Great Northern	auger
planter	bean cutter

About the Authors and Illustrator

Carole Amateis lives on a farm near Bridgeport, Nebraska, with her husband, Mike where they raised three children. She has five grandchildren, is a long-time Sunday School teacher, youth choir director and piano teacher. She has eight years experience as a newspaper reporter, composes music, is an avid photographer, and currently editor of "The Bean Bag", a publication of the Nebraska Dry Bean Growers Association.

Melissa Amateis-Marsh resides in Gering, Nebraska, with her husband, Ron, and family. She holds a bachelor of arts degree in history and English from Chadron State College. She loves to travel, read, and is currently at work on her novel and other literary endeavors.

Randy Sides lives in Bayard, Nebraska, with his wife, Jennifer, and three-year-old daughter, Syrena. He has an associate of science degree from Western Nebraska Community College. He enjoys art, music, sports, and computers. This book has renewed his passion for drawing.

This book was produced as a promotional project by:
Nebraska Dry Bean Commission
4502 Avenue I, Scottsbluff, Nebraska, 69361
(308) 632-1258.
Email: office@nebraskadrybean.com
Web Site: www.nebraskadrybean.com

For additional copies for educational purposes, contact the Nebraska Dry Bean Commission at:

4502 Avenue I, Scottsbluff, Nebraska, 69361
(308) 632-1258
Email: office@nebraskadrybean.com
Web Site: www.nebraskadrybean.com

If you would like to order additional copies of <u>Benjamin Bean: Planting, Growing, Harvesting</u> please send the completed order form with payment to:

Benjamin Productions
c/o Carole Amateis
Rt. 2 Box 77B
Broadwater, NE 69125

Teacher's guides are also available.

Please send me additional copies of <u>Benjamin Bean: Planting, Growing, Harvesting</u>

NAME_____

ADDRESS_____

_____

\# Of Books____ @ $6.95 each = $_____.____

\# of Teacher's Guides ____ @ $4.95 each = $_____.____

Plus Shipping fee (book)   + $2.00
Plus Shipping fee (guide)   + $1.00

TOTAL ENCLOSED $_____